THE
BURNING BUSH
STILL SPEAKS

THE
BURNING BUSH
STILL SPEAKS

SALLY - ANN MARTIN

authorHOUSE®

AuthorHouse™ UK Ltd.
1663 Liberty Drive
Bloomington, IN 47403 USA
www.authorhouse.co.uk
Phone: 0800.197.4150

Published by AuthorHouse   09/09/2013

ISBN: 978-1-4918-7804-0 (sc)
ISBN: 978-1-4918-7805-7 (e)

Any people depicted in stock imagery provided by Thinkstock are models,
and such images are being used for illustrative purposes only.
Certain stock imagery © Thinkstock.

This book is printed on acid-free paper.

Because of the dynamic nature of the Internet, any web addresses or
links contained in this book may have changed since publication and
may no longer be valid. The views expressed in this work are solely those
of the author and do not necessarily reflect the views of the publisher,
and the publisher hereby disclaims any responsibility for them.

CONTENTS

Foreword vii

Chapter One 1
Chapter Two 5
Chapter Three 9
Chapter Four 15
Chapter Five 23
Chapter Six 30
Chapter Seven 37
Chapter Eight 42
Chapter Nine 47
Chapter Ten 55
Chapter Eleven 62
Chapter Twelve 69

Foreword

"*What is it that causes a young woman to leave her studies at university and start working in the children's homes of Pretoria? Sally sums it up beautifully for us, "When God called me up for this ministry, I was single, and ready for marriage and raising a family. I am also an extrovert, good at making speeches and debating. God knew this. He knew that others couldn't do what I could, and needed a voice. Not only was He opening a door for the ministry of the Scriptures, but those whom were under-privileged were finally going to meet someone that had a very loud voice, and didn't give up . . . who endured. Also, the Lord was teaching me humility. I had everything at my disposal, and I was entering a world of hardship, neglect, abuse and injustice." The answer to my question, is God. It is only He that calls people from the ordinary into something extraordinary, and that is certainly how I would describe Sally's story 'Extraordinary!' Moses had an encounter with God at a burning bush in Exodus 3. There God commanded Him to take off his sandals for the place he was standing on was holy ground. He commissions Moses, despite his protests, to go back to Egypt and tell Pharaoh to let His people go. As a sign that God went with him, the staff in his hand would be used by God to do wondrous miracles. The biblical story is well known, but Sally in these pages, encourages us to believe in more 'Burning Bush' encounters.*

What you are about to read is a wonderful reminder that God not only calls ordinary people, like you and me, to do the extraordinary, but when He calls he also equips and meets our every need. Sally's story is remarkable, founding a charity, finding desperate teenagers, seeing lives utterly transformed and renewed. Yet perhaps the greatest journey in this story is the one Sally herself takes. I wholly recommend this book to you. It is a story of faith, courage, and seeing God work in amazing ways, leaving us wondering "does He still work in these ways today? Does he still speak, does He still preform miracles through His people?" Sally's answer is an emphatic YES! God still answers prayer, God still works miracles, God still takes ordinary people, like Sally, and uses them to do extraordinary things.

Read on and be encouraged, but also be challenged. The question Sally asks, and we all must answer, is what will your response be when God asks you to do something, to stand up for, to speak out for, to stand with, the poor, the needy, the forgotten, the broken. What will your answer be?

**Rev Neil Bennett CertTh, DipCoun, DipTh, BTh
Team Leader: Ross-on-Wye Baptist Church**

Chapter One

JUST LOOK!

When I look back at my life, I can truly say that God still works miracles today, as He did back in the days of the Bible. So many people want proof that God exists. They try to prove His existence through science, technology, and astronomy, but no one has just looked at the miracles God has created in the lives of those He has used. I know, because as soon as I allowed the Lord to start working in my life, I could truly see what Moses, Joseph, Daniel, and Elijah probably saw. No, I wasn't thrown into a lion's den, but I came jolly close. I can relate to Joseph, when I remember my rebelliousness and the magnificence of God's miracles later. God can also get "with it"; you just have to let Him.

I remember a song my nursery school teacher taught us:

> I'm a brave, brave mouse,
> I go marching through the house,
> And I'm not afraid of anything.

> For danger I'm prepared,
> And I'm never, never scared,
> No, I'm not afraid of anything!

This is always the attitude of a university student. Bring—it—on! I'm not scared of anything. I think the Lord used this attitude to His advantage. I went to church one Sunday, and a missionary was sharing with the Church about all the trials and tribulations she was going through in her work, but, on the same note, the absolute *joy* she was experiencing in seeing God work through her and save people's lives. I was jealous. Why was God only using selected people and not me? Was there a degree you had to get? Was there an age limit? Then it struck me. I hadn't gone on my knees and made myself available to Him. That night I prayed and said to God that I would even smuggle Bibles to China if He needed me to. I would also go to Hungary if need be. I think He just smiled and said, "Okay, I'll use you, but I need you right here in this city."

> The word of the Lord came to me saying: "Before I formed you in the womb I knew you. Before you were born I set you apart; I appointed you as a prophet to the nations."
>
> "Ah Sovereign Lord', I said, "I do not know how to speak, I am only a child." (Jeremiah 1:4-6)

Jeremiah was "appointed" by God as a prophet to the nations. God has a purpose for each Christian, but some people are appointed by God for specific kinds of work. Samson, David, John the Baptist, Jonah, and Paul are all examples of people who were called to do particular jobs for God. If God gives you a specific task, accept it cheerfully, and do it with diligence. If God has not given you a specific task or assignment, then seek to fulfil the mission common to all believers—to love, obey, and serve God, until His guidance becomes clear.

Endurance is not a common quality. Many people lack the long-term commitment, caring, and willingness that are vital to sticking with a task against all odds. Jeremiah was a prophet who endured.

Many "gods" entice us to turn away from ministry and God. Material possessions, career choices, the approval of others, family, the wrong friends, and incorrect goals compete for our total commitment.

Jeremiah's call from God teaches how intimately God knows us. He valued us before anyone else knew we would exist. He planned our lives whilst our bodies were still being formed, and He values us more highly than we value ourselves.

When God called me up for this ministry, I was single and ready to get married and raise a family. I am also an extrovert, good at making speeches and debating. God knew this. He knew that others couldn't do what I could, and He needed a voice. Not only was He opening a door for the ministry of the scriptures, but those who were under-privileged were finally going to meet someone that had a very loud voice, someone who didn't give up, but endured. Also, the Lord was teaching me humility. I had everything at my disposal, and I was entering a world of hardship, neglect, abuse, and injustice.

What I also didn't know was that I would be taking on nine children as my own and raising them all alone. Even though I was earning a small salary at a recently acquired job to stay above board, I was enduring medical hardships, but the Lord *always* provided shelter, food, transportation, medication, clothing, and enough money through the strangest donations, so that His will could be done. Not only could I keep an eye on nine children, but these kids would marry and turn Christmas into a head-count of eighteen. Then, they began their own families, and the family God blessed me with became enormous!

God knew my needs. Through the years as the children got older and had different requirements, they became more and more expensive to have around, but God always provided in some way—by an increase in income, new careers, tax returns—the list is endless. I had a job to do for God, and God made it happen. I just had to stop and listen.

Chapter Two

GETTING OFF THE BLOCK

The Lord laid it upon my heart to start working in the children's homes in Pretoria. I quit my studies at university, got a job at one of the major banks in South Africa, and started finding out where all the children's homes were.

I found two children's homes to begin with. My friend and I went to see the home parents and social workers, and they didn't see a problem with us taking the teenagers out for the day. This carried on for a while, but we noticed the kids weren't really communicating with us. When we asked them what was wrong, they said that one afternoon out wasn't enough, they wanted a weekend away. That meant a camp. That meant money, food, and transportation. This would take planning. However, we planned a camp for forty teenagers for four days at one of the Scripture Union base camps. The children's homes couldn't pay for the camps, so somehow we would have to find the funds to cover the costs.

This caused me enormous anxiety. To me, raising R9000.00 was almost the same as asking me to run the Comrades' Marathon. My father noticed this concern; without my knowledge he contacted his business partners, and they started paying in cheques from all their businesses. In two weeks, camp, food and transport were paid for. There was even money left over to buy prizes and medicines, as well as art and sports equipment. Just a few balls and paint brushes, but hey, it was more than we bargained for!

We went to camp and had the time of our lives. So many people back home didn't believe that we could accomplish this, and when the bus brought us back that late Sunday afternoon—a bus full of singing, rowdy teens—it opened the eyes of many adults that God was at work, and a new chapter was about to unfold.

> When John heard in prison what Christ was doing, he sent his disciples to ask him, "Are you the one who was to come, or should we expect someone else?" Jesus replied, "Go back and report to John what you hear and see. The blind receive sight, the lame walk, those who have leprosy are cured, the deaf hear, the dead are raised, and the good news is preached to the poor. Blessed is the man who does not fall away on account of me." (Matthew 11:2-6)

As John sat in prison, he began to have doubts about whether Jesus really was the Messiah. Jesus answered John's doubts by pointing to Jesus's acts of healing, raising the dead, and preaching good news to the poor. With so much evidence, Jesus's identity was obvious. If you sometimes doubt your salvation or even God's work in your life, just look at the evidence of the scriptures, and then think how God changed your life.

I had made mistakes here. I had doubted that we would reach the financial target, I had doubted that we would have a successful camp, and I had forgotten that God was in control, not me.

Ten children gave their lives to Christ at that camp, and I became known as Auntie Sally amongst the kids and the children's homes from then on.

We had been the first group not to drop or disappoint the children for a number of years, and it was now up to us to keep up the target that we had set. Camp would now be an annual event every April during the school holidays.

One thing my mother got right with me was insisting that I read a lot. I will always love and be grateful to her for that. Readers are leaders. I had oodles of fiction books from the past, and they had created an *imagination* in me. Imagination had created a theme for next year's camp. Imagination foresees what can be, but then you have to call a meeting with your team and ask the more practical players, "Is this possible?" The dreamers, like myself, are the ones who plan camps and think about the themes that they create. We are the recipes for the future youth planning. The more cynical people look at what we have thought about, and eighty per cent of the time our ideas get passed. Sometimes we dream too high, our ideas are too expensive, or the teenagers won't be able to make the target physically. Most of the time it's up to us to think, or nothing will ever happen. In the book of Dr Seuss:

> Waiting for a fish to bite,
> Or waiting for wind to fly a kite,
> Or waiting around for Friday night,
> Or waiting perhaps for their Uncle Jake.

Waiting for what? For the kids to grow up? For me to get married and have children of my own? By then it's too late! The time is now! Those children needed me *then*, and I had to act. Even if it meant foregoing my entire career, I knew God would look after me, and look after me He did.

Another reason I just dropped out of university and went into charity work was because I was "burning with fire". As David Brainerd so avidly put it:

> Oh, that I might be a flaming fire in the service
> of the Lord. Here I am, Lord, send me, send me
> to the ends of the earth send me from all that is
> called earthly comfort, send me even to death
> itself if it be, but in Thy service and to promote
> Thy kingdom.

After the success of the camp, I knew God would be there for camp number two. The kids had absolutely "lit up" at camp, and we had become close to them. However, playing a few games wasn't going to cut it. We needed something that would make them think, something competitive, something that they could take back to the children's homes and never forget spiritually.

I had a lot of reading to do.

Chapter Three

MORE MIRACLES

After the success we had with the children with at our first camp, we were told that the laws had changed in the country, and if we were to survive as a charity, we had to comply. We made an appointment with the attorneys, where the correct papers were drawn up registering us as a formal charity in South Africa with the name of Teens Bridge.

After that it was off to the auditors to let them know that we were in town, and, God-willing, the firm we approached didn't have a charity, so they agreed to audit our books for free. Another miracle!

We then all had to go to the bank and open a new bank account with everyone's signatures. The last stop was registering Teens Bridge at the Department of Welfare for a charity number. Without the number we were forbidden to raise money or ask for any sort of welfare. Thankfully, the number was granted, and we continued with God's work.

This time around, I had found two more children's homes. We calculated that with two extra homes, camp would consist of about sixty children. We drew up some very official-looking forms. We had done our homework and had learnt that children had to be signed off by social workers; you couldn't just whisk them away. We also needed to know what medication any of the kids were on, as we had been hearing by the wayside that some of the children took medicine.

So with childlike faith I was sauntering on, thinking "Dad's buddies" could help again. You can imagine my horror when two hundred applications for camp were returned to me. Two hundred!

My father contributed a mere ten per cent of the money, and the food list was as long as my arm! Ninety chickens, one hundred loaves of bread, and one hundred litres of milk were required by the cook. The list was endless. It just wasn't possible. I went to my bedroom and burst into tears. This wasn't in my plan. My plan had been sixty kids, and Dad would help—simple! But now I had been given an enormous figure, which was just too high to reach. The worst thing was that I was embarrassed. I didn't know how to live up to it. How was I going to tell two hundred kids that camp was off?

I confided in an elder in the Church, and he told me he would make a few phone calls. What good would that do? He was as old as the ark, didn't work anymore, and didn't have much money, but I had to be polite, pray with him, and say thanks. You can imagine my surprise when this old man phoned to say that all the camp fees had been taken care of!

I nearly fainted to the floor. He might have been very old, but it turned out that he sat on one of the bank's trusts. A client had, in his will, left his millions to all children's charity work in South Africa, and this particular bank was the executor of his estate. Every year they would decide which charity would get cheques from this deceased man's account, and thanks to the elder in my Church and to God sitting in at the meeting, we got R40 000,00. That was quite a step up from the R9 000,00 we had received the year before!

However, my problems were still not over. The money would pay for the children's accommodation, transport, prizes, artwork, outdoor entertainment, and the like, but I still had that food list, and the date for camp was drawing nearer and nearer. Did I give the R40 000,00 back to the trust and call camp off, or did I trust God? I chose the latter. I got down on my knees again and prayed. I said to God that He had blessed us so abundantly, He had given us money, He had granted all the leaders leave from work, and we had an enormous turn-out from the kids, please, would He help us in finding the food.

I wanted to go to Church and just find comfort within the walls of the Church. My team and I asked the pastor if we could just make an announcement from the pulpit. He agreed. We told the congregation how things were progressing, and we asked if they wanted to assist in any way, could they contribute by just purchasing a litre of milk and a chicken. This sounded so stupid! Can we please have a litre of milk and a chicken?

After the service, an old lady came to me and said that she would donate one whole chicken and a litre of milk. Well, that was eighty-nine chickens to go, and ninety-nine litres of milk. Swell! As I reached the car, I could feel tears in my eyes. I knew that on Monday I would have to cancel camp. As I was about to get in, a stranger approached me and said, "Fax me your list." He pressed a paper with a fax number into my hand. I insisted that I just wanted the milk and the chickens, as this list was endless. He smiled and said, "Fax me your list," and was gone.

Well, I thought, if you want to see my list and collapse, that's fine with me. I faxed the list. No one phoned. I was beginning to panic, as camp was drawing closer and closer and I didn't know what to do. Eventually, while I was sitting at work, trying to concentrate, I got a call from the Church. Apparently, trucks and trucks of food had rolled up from nowhere and were unloading food into the hall, the freezers—just almost everywhere. There was so much food that the houses next door had to assist with their deep freezers and fridges as well. When I got to the Church, my mouth hung open when I saw what God had done. It was just food, food, food! We had prayed for food, and we got food! The entire list was complete, except for the bread. That we had to buy with the money that we had received.

Once again I had doubted, but God had provided. Camp was on!

> Elijah said to her, "Don't be afraid. Go home and do as you have said. But first make a small cake of bread for me from what you have and bring it to me, and then make something for yourself and your son. For this is what the Lord, the God of Israel says: 'The jar of flour will not

be used up and the jug of oil will not run dry
until the day the Lord gives rain on the land.'"
(1 Kings 17:13-14)

It turned out that the total stranger was a visitor to my
Church that night and that the Lord had laid it upon his
heart to assist us. His job was in the food export business,
so to phone his friends and ask for assistance regarding fish,
Vienna's, chickens, meat, milk, eggs, vegetables, and fruit
was easy. He and I kept this relationship up for another ten
years and another ten camps, just like the woman with the
flour and the oil. The Bank trust kept sending R40 000,00
every year, even after the elder of the Church had passed
away. The children wrote "thank you" notes to these specific
donors year after year, and God's work just flourished.

Doing God's work does put one on a road of insecurity.
There is no guaranteed salary, no job to go to every day.
Everything is unexpected. So there will be anxiety in the
beginning. However, God teaches us to trust Him, and to
depend on Him rather than on others.

Philippians 4:19 teaches "My God will meet all your needs
according to His glorious riches in Christ Jesus."

Lessons we can learn from this are:

- God is all I need.
- Where God guides, He always provides.
- I must trust Him one day at a time.
- God's promises hinge on my obedience.
- I don't give to get a blessing, but to be a blessing.

> Then the word of the Lord came to Elijah:
> "Leave here, turn eastward and hide in the
> Kerith Ravine, east of the Jordan. You will
> drink from the brook, and I have ordered the
> ravens to feed you there." (1 Kings 17:2-4)

In a nation that was required by law to care for its prophets, it is ironic that God turned to ravens (unclean birds) to care for Elijah. God has help where we least expect it. He provides for us in ways that go beyond our narrow definitions or expectations. No matter how bitter our trials or how seemingly hopeless our situation, we should look to God for His caring touch. We may find His providence in some strange places!

Chapter Four

GOD IN CONTROL

As you can well imagine, the children were most excited about camp. I was a bit nervous, as I had never been responsible for so many children plus a team before. Yet I had that comfort in my heart that if God had provided all the necessary for camp, He would be *at* camp too!

My theme for that year was "Somewhere over the Rainbow". Our artists had drawn huge rainbows with pots of gold at the end, and we divided the children into teams and named them the Red, Green, Orange, Blue, Yellow, Purple, Black, and Brown teams. This way, discipline could easily be enforced, because if one teenager was punished, the whole team got penalised. The teams took this very seriously, as camp was all about winning at the end. It got to such an extreme that kids would start mopping floors, washing our cars, picking up litter, just to earn extra points for their teams. I don't think the campsites have *ever* been so well looked after and so clean before. It also taught them time management. When we started playing the music, it meant "Come to the hall." The last one in got his team penalised!

The kids had workbooks which they had to work through every day, and in the books I had researched all the colours and what they meant. I had worked out crosswords and word-finders for them, and I didn't say a word about what prize lay in store for the person who bothered to do these.

I had flown in books from the United States for myself to read and to get ideas for camp. The thought of two hundred kids playing cricket for a week wasn't going to suffice. We needed more difficult things for them to do. Some of the ideas we found in the books did amuse us greatly. We had brought big refrigerator boxes to camp, and the children had to jump in the boxes and race against one another in these things. From a distance this could be very entertaining, seeing black and white legs running on the green grass, with a big box strapped over their bodies. They enjoyed it; it was something they didn't do every day back at the children's home.

We gave them a cake race. Beautifully decorated cakes were bought from the shops, and each team had to take their cake through the most difficult obstacle courses. We then judged the cakes at the end of the race to see which team's cake still looked the best and which team's time was the shortest.

To complicate things a bit more, each team had to walk five miles to a different base camp and spend the night there. They had to take their own wood, water, sleeping bags, and food. I had combined different boxes of food for them. One night, a team would get foil, flour, cabbage, and sausages. They had to work out their own menus using the ingredients in the box the utensils supplied. They would try to assist the other teams by telling them to take can openers, not knowing I had changed the menus. The next team would get fresh fish, pineapples, biscuits, and potatoes. This way, they had to figure out how to cook their own food using water and a camp fire. They had to be sensible and go sleep early, and not sit and talk the whole night. However, we had taken their security away. There was no warmth of a bed anymore, no toilet, and no warm meal like all the others were getting. Their entertainment was each other, not the fun going on in the hall, and they knew it.

But these kids had to start understanding that life was like that. Once they reached eighteen years of age, they would be asked to leave the children's home, so that a younger child could have their bed. They would have to survive. We were teaching them how. We were also teaching them that no matter where they were, God would be with them.

We also sent them to the dam for the day. Here they were given six barrels and some rope and were ordered to build a boat. If they felt their boat was stable, they all had to get on it and row to the other side. The boys (as usual) wouldn't take any tips or hints from the girls. They knew what they were doing! Once the boats hit the water, we could see that two of them were going to fall apart. The whole lot of them fell into the dam, barrels and all. I don't think I've ever seen boys get such a good thumping as they did that day, because they didn't "listen".

Those are memories that I can look back at and smile at. However, the Devil also came to camp. One of the social workers forgot to pack the medication for one of the children, and he just "lost it". He ran out of the camp grounds, and before we knew it, his adrenaline was so high that he was scampering down the highway! Now this child was black, and I'm white. He was a young kid, while I haven't run since my schooldays, which were thirty-odd years ago. Lord, where are you? This child can't have a seizure on me! I don't know where I got this energy, but I was after him in a flash. You can imagine the amazement of all the drivers on the highway—this white woman running after this little black boy! I almost had him, I promise! He just was too quick. Eventually, I stood still on the highway and forced a BMW to come to a stop. "Follow that child," I panted. "He needs medication." The driver assisted, and with his help we got him to a hospital. I phoned the children's home from there, and the doctors injected him with the medication he required. I was given the pills from the hospital, and the driver gave us a lift back to camp. I was sunburnt and could hardly walk. My legs had been given such a wake-up call! I just wanted to take a shower to cool off and to go sit quietly in my room and reflect on what had happened.

Why did God allow things like that? Didn't God want camp to be a success? I had hardly had time to finish a cold drink when a member of my team burst into my room to tell me that one of the children had fallen and possibly broken her neck. All the blood drained from my face. I couldn't believe this. I ran outside. A girl had been playing on the jungle gym, when someone yanked the rope and she fell. All the girls were screaming, hyperventilating, and causing panic. Camp had to go on. A few smacks here and there, a shout or two, and order was restored. The ambulance fetched the young lass, and I ordered two of my team to go with her to the hospital. We, as a camp, prayed for her, but the children knew I was angry. I think my face gives me away. They were told to carry on with their arts and crafts for another two hours, because I needed peace and quiet.

After an hour, my cell phone rang to say that the young girl was okay—that she wasn't paralyzed or anything awful, just numb. The doctors were working with her, and she would be coming back to camp with my team leaders. I just sank to my knees again and thanked God for His goodness and protection from evil.

They say trouble always comes in threes. Well, we had the adrenaline boy and the jungle-gym girl. What would be next? At supper we were relaxing and looking forward to the evening's events when we heard yet another scream. Another young girl's throat was swelling and swelling, and she could hardly breathe or speak. My team just threw her in the car and whisked her off to the doctor down the road. Luckily, she was back in an hour. No one from the children's home told us she was allergic to fish, and here we were all happily eating pilchards for supper, herself included.

I was ready to pack my bags and walk all the way home! I didn't sign up for this! I came from a bank environment, where everything was done in an orderly manner and no surprises came at you through the back door. Camp was supposed to be orderly. I had arranged schedules, workbooks, times, dates, and places. Everything was orderly.

What I forgot was that this wasn't the bank, and even it had been the bank, even banks get hit by recessions which they don't see coming. Missionary work isn't orderly. It's one surprise after another. It can be a nice surprise, or a downright awful one. It all depends on how you handle it.

> Then Samson prayed unto the Lord: "O Sovereign Lord, remember me. O God, strengthen me just once more, and let me with one blow get revenge on the Philistines for my two eyes." Then Samson reached toward the two central pillars on which the temple stood. Bracing himself against them, his right hand on the one, and his left hand on the other, Samson said, "Let me die with the Philistines!" Then he pushed with all his might, and down came the temple on the rulers and all the people in it. (Judges 16: 28-30)

The Teens Bridge team had taken three knocks on the chin, but that did not mean that God's work was stopping. The lad that headed the art department called me and showed me a series of artworks. I saw a picture of a young girl trapped in a jail cell with a ball and chain on her foot. When I asked her about it, it came out that her entire family was bipolar, and they relied on her to take care of them. She was now the "mother" of the house. After camp was over, we visited this house and, to our horror, realised it didn't even have a front door. Althea had to cook, clean, and look after her mother, older brother, sister, and baby brother. Her love was art. She so wanted to draw. Eventually we put her in art school to finish her education, and the rest of the family received the care they needed. It all began at camp.

I became fond of several children, and I came to realise that one of them, Joos, had been sexually molested within the children's Home. He, along with thirteen other children, had been violated, but the abuser had threatened them so much that they were all too scared to say anything. Joos wrote a statement at camp which we faxed to the police, and we took further action, wanting to know why the social workers didn't know anything. We realised now that camp wasn't just camp; it had become a haven where teenagers were opening up to us. This would require extra training, manpower, and support.

Even though camp had now forced Teens Bridge to become a serious charity to protect the welfare of minors, I still encouraged the children to dream and to use their imaginations. Many of them had an understanding that after school all they were good enough for was to go work at the local pet shop and earn a few rand to stay alive. After all, they were kids from a children's home; they weren't upper class and rich.

The older ones had started to notice that I never drove a car to the homes and that only my friends did. They decided to find out why. When they asked, it was a case of "Do I tell them or don't I?" I decided they were old enough to understand my secrets, and I explained to them that the reason that I never drove a car was because I suffered from epilepsy. Even though I had wealthy parents, I didn't have my health like they did.

This startled the children quite a bit, as they had put me on a pedestal—perfect home, perfect future, and perfect health. They never realised how many secrets I was actually carrying around. The Lord has allowed epilepsy to come into my life since I was five years old, and when I was eighteen, like everyone else, I so wanted to drive. However, my parents and neurologist couldn't allow it because of the impact it might have should I have an attack behind the wheel of a car. Year after year I travelled by bus to work, thinking that God despised me, not realising that this was how God was building my imagination. I could remember street names for car rallies, I could see what was being built where, and in the bus I had all the time in the world to sit back, relax, and plan the following year's camp.

As Judy Garland so beautifully put it:

> Somewhere, over the rainbow,
> Way up high,
> There's a land that I heard of once
> In a lullaby.

These words can make a person think of an imaginary place, or one can really imagine what heaven will look like. What will all the characters of the Bible look like? What will their personalities be like? One day, when I cross over that rainbow to meet my Saviour, I'd like to know that those children will be coming as well and that my dreamy imagination wasn't for nothing.

Chapter Five

MAKE A JOYFUL NOISE!

Camp carried on year after year. Every April we received our cheque for R40 000,00 from the bank trust, and I would fax the food list to the "Food Man". As sure as nuts, those lorries would roll in the week camp was about to start, filled to the brim with the required food. God looked after the accommodation, food, transport, medication, prizes, and even Bible distribution. We had money to print our workbooks, the pamphlets that were advertising camp, *and* there was money left over for when we returned.

I started remembering the story of Joseph a lot here, when God provided food for the Egyptians and Joseph was made second in charge to Pharaoh.

> Joseph was thirty years old when he entered the service of Pharaoh the king of Egypt. And Joseph went out from Pharaoh's presence and travelled throughout Egypt. During the seven years of abundance the land produced

> plentifully. Joseph collected all the food
> produced in those seven years of abundance in
> Egypt and stored it in the cities. In each city he
> put the food grown in the fields surrounding
> it. Joseph stored up huge quantities of grain,
> like the sand of the sea; it was so much that he
> stopped keeping records because it was beyond
> measure. (Genesis 41: 46-49)

I can relate to Joseph here. First, I had to make notes to always thank the bank trust for the R40 000,00 that came consistently every year, and I know they enjoyed the children's "thank you" letters. Then, I had to write and thank the "Food Man" and all his friends. The kids thought the food in camp was fantastic, so he really got a lot of mail. *A lot!* As a friend of mine once said, "Well Sal, your food must have been fantastic, for the kids keep talking about food, food, food all the time."

I started taking chances by writing to big retail shops and industrial warehouses, not thinking that I would get any reply. Imagine my surprise when I came home from work and saw the outside spare room and bathroom piled to the roof full of chocolate! I only requested a few slabs for prizes. These guys didn't muck around, they sent an entire container! I would be dreaming about chocolate for the next year. And it did last for an entire year.

A friend and I decided we were going to try and get the local shop just to donate bread. With these we would make hotdogs, and we would save a few rand by using this procedure. We found a manager. He put all the hotdog rolls in a trolley and asked us if we needed anything else. We said yes. We started packing the Vienna's, mustard, tomato sauce, plates, margarine, and cold drinks, as this was what we were going to pay for. God really does know how to smack me. The manager wheeled the entire trolley out of the shop and straight to the car. We paid *nothing*! He was in a good mood that day, so we got the deal for free. Believe me, Joseph and I are going to chat.

I had also written to another retail store asking for toys, as I thought it would be cute if we could, as a team, wrap a few toys for Christmas and give them to all the little kids. The big kids always got camp, but the little ones always missed out. Well, as usual I got caught with my foot in it, for a huge lorry pulled up at the front door wanting to know where it could off-load all these toys. Believe me, we were wrapping, and wrapping. I wanted a Christmas, I got a Christmas!

I've always loved knitting. Never sit idle. However, buying wool for all those kids can be pretty costly. I therefore phoned the wool factory to see what my chances were. Let's just say that when they were finished with me, we needed a new house. I really didn't have room anymore.

The way God bestowed His blessings, not just on me and my team but on the children was absolutely phenomenal, and it showed me that God can still work miracles today. He hasn't parted a sea for me or spoken to me from a burning bush, but oh my, has He done it the modern way! He has told me via money and food that He wanted a camp on an annual basis, and every year two hundred children arrived. When we needed a few slabs of chocolate, He sent a year's supply. He also looked after the little ones by means of bestowing toys on them for Christmas and giving them a December to remember! And now he was laughing at me by sending me enough wool to keep me busy till I'm sixty-five. With all this wool we were able to get old-age homes busy with the project so that blankets could be made for the poor.

What is most incredible about God is that during all these miracles I was working in a bank that had very strict rules. No personal phone calls or e-mails were allowed, nor any personal visitors. Banking was about getting the statistics out, and they had better be correct. All this other "stuff" had to be done in my spare time. Yet even with my measly salary and with no husband, I still survived every month even after the medical aid had swallowed half my salary for the tablets I needed.

The Lord touched the life of a young man named Anthony. Anthony was very driven and keen to serve God, and he was full of that "burning fire" that I had felt and seen in myself many years ago. Anthony is a black chap, so ministering to the little ones in the rural areas seemed to be Anthony's calling. I was sitting at work one day after camp was finished, when Anthony burst into the bank. Somehow the kids got past security; I don't what they said to the guards, but they got to my offices. Anthony came rushing in and wanted my credit card. I asked him what for. He said that his little group had started with only six children, so he made the fatal mistake of making them lunch. Word spread, and now about sixty little children were walking miles in the summer sun just for the food. Their parents were so poor that when they heard Anthony had food, they would get up early in the morning when

it was still cool and start to walk with no shoes on their feet. By the time they got to Anthony, they were ready to faint because of exhaustion, dehydration, and hunger. I knew the shop over the road wouldn't bother to check that I was white and female while Anthony was black and male, so I gave him the card. He went and got all the necessary supplies, jumped into a taxi, and headed back to his rural area out in the townships. Today, loads of children still come to Anthony's school, and after he has fed them, he tells them all the Bible stories we all heard when we were four or five.

> If one of you says to him, "Go, I wish you well, keep warm and well fed," but does nothing about his physical needs, what good is it? In the same way, faith by itself, if it is not accompanied by action, it is dead. (James 2:16)

In the same way, is it too much to ask that we should help those who don't have what we have or just be nice to people? When did you last visit someone in an old-age home or just make a hospital visit? There are so many folk who need assistance crossing the street or help with their packets. Did you help today? I used to catch that bus much against my will, but a blind man used to get on. He was an engineer, so he wasn't stupid or incapable, but the bus would come to a stop at a double carriage way, and he would need someone to help him across the road. Back in South Africa there are no buttons on robots for the pedestrians to press. There it's a ready, *go!* For a blind person this is not so simple. God used me to take that man to his work every morning. Sometimes the bus forgot to stop, and someone would have to have the courage to scream "Stop!"

from the back of the bus. Otherwise this engineer would wind up somewhere he didn't want to be.

Another woman and I were the two disciplinarians on that bus. Any young person who was too loud for our ears got a crack with the newspaper, and if that didn't work, he got removed from the bus by bodily force at the next bus stop. We didn't allow old people to stand whilst young people sat or ladies to stand whilst men sat. No, no. Etiquette was followed on that bus, but it was all enforced with a smile and a newspaper.

These days I see people walking around with very serious faces looking as though they have just heard some awful news. People never smile any more. What folk have to understand is that children watch you all the time. They read you like a book. When you are grumpy and cross all the time, the child isn't going to come and tell you about his or her day or about a problem in his or her life. I'm not saying you should wear a clown suit and pretend that life is a bunch of roses, but when things are going well, at least tell someone and share your good news. Tell those around you how you got complimented at work. Tell those around you that you got an increase in pay. Tell those around you that that you got picked for the team. It makes such a difference to children when they see and pick up positivity. Like Anthony, it affects how they turn out in the end.

Smile (From *Chicken Soup for the Teenage Soul*)

> She smiled at a sorrowful stranger.
> The smile seemed to make him feel better.
> He remembered past kindnesses from a friend,

"That never cost a cent" are the most important words in the entire poem. It costs nothing to be nice and courteous to someone. It costs nothing to smile at someone when entering a room or when meeting someone for the first time. Many folk are in deep depression; some are even contemplating suicide. Imagine them seeing a cheery face that shows them God loves them and that life isn't as bad as it seems. If those children from the children's homes, who were physically or sexually abused or who had lost their parents, can make it, why can't you?

Chapter Six

BRINGING OUT THE TALENTS

The biggest mistake I made with the children was thinking that they would always remain in the homes. Life would just carry on, we would just continue with our camps, and everyone would leave us alone.

I didn't notice that the kids were getting older, that they were reaching their final years of schooling. Whilst I was sitting at work one day, the door opened and three of the children ran in with a look of total devastation on their faces. They had been studying for their finals, when a social worker, not thinking, walked in on them and told them that they only had thirty days left in the home. Their beds had already been allocated to new children, and they must please start thinking about new places of residence.

Apparently there was a huge uproar at the home. The final Science exam was the next day, and these kids were worrying about survival, not their studies. I had to get them to go back to their rooms and concentrate, and believe me, the home got a quite a phone call from me! Once again, we had a new problem. As before, I turned to the Lord. "Lord, you know we can't throw these kids onto the street where drugs and prostitution are everywhere. Please open someone's heart to help us here."

I took this to the Church, and within the required period we found a "nature course" that the kids could be sent on. Each child would cost R3000,00. If I could find the sponsors, at least the kids would have shelter, food, and an education, and I would have time to find them a more permanent place to stay.

God in His love spoke again to the people at the Church, and we got the number of cheques for R3000,00 that were required to send the children away for three months. They had peace of mind knowing that they wouldn't land up on the streets. This news brought comfort to the students, and they put all their effort into their final exams. When the results came out in the newspapers the following January, every one of them had passed! I don't know if it was their fear of me or God's grace that got them through, but looking at their results, I saw hard work and determination on all their papers. My kids had done it!

However, I realised my "kids" had now grown up. They were liable now for drivers' licences, they could vote, they would probably fall in love soon, and get married. Were camp days over? Not for these children. They had loved camp so much that they wanted camp to carry on, as long as they could be leaders this time around. They knew the rules, and they could also see that I was getting tired and needed assistance. Teens Bridge had grown!

I was flattered that the children wanted to assist with the camps, but they needed a "mom" in their lives. The Child Care law had expired, they were over eighteen years of age now, not minors anymore. I could actually do what I wanted to with them now! I saw that kids from the children's homes always underestimated themselves and never lived up to their true potential. So now it was up to me to drop kick the potential I was seeing into some of them!

Pieter had been cycling to school for years and was very fit. His "buddy" Joos also enjoyed cycling. So out of my savings I bought bicycles for these two. They were thrilled! What they didn't know is that a woman always has a hidden agenda. We don't buy things like a bicycle unless it's for some big target at the end! I had entered these two in the Pick 'n' Pay 94.7 Challenge, which takes place every November in South Africa, one of our hottest months. A contact of mine had spoken to Hollard Insurance, which supplied us with helmets, gear, and sponsorship. The boys were speechless. They tried to get out of the race, but my deal with them was that if they could cycle this race in under four hours, I would fly them to Cape Town so that they could do the Argus the following year. The deal was on! I waited at the finish line for my kids, not thinking they would make the cut-off time for the Argus. After all, they only had bicycles, not racing bikes! God probably peeped out of heaven and put energy into Pieter's and Joos's legs, because those two came across the finish line in three hours and twenty minutes. I guess I had some planning to do!

We still don't know who was more surprised—me or Pieter and Joos. They doubted that they could finish the race, but now they had just raised the stakes, as the Argus had called them up to take part due to their good times. I managed to get us a place to stay with family in Cape Town, and I kept my word by flying them to Cape Town the next year. They were so excited, as aeroplanes weren't a common sight for them. Also, they had never seen Cape Town! Here they got to cycle up the most beautiful mountain in the world and look down on the Atlantic Ocean as they pedalled. I also bought them two racing bikes this time, since they had earned their place in the cycling world. At the finish line, Pieter's time was remarkably good, and he has qualified to do the Tour de France. He hasn't done it yet, and it is up to him now to raise his own money and set his own travel arrangements. My biggest problem was in November that year for the second Pick 'n' Pay 94.7 Challenge: having seen the fun Pieter and Joos had had, thirteen kids now wanted to take part. I entered all thirteen, and all of them finished the race. Not in the required time for the Argus, but they had that will and determination to finish!

Pieter's brother Josef was always a very good-looking young man. I had always heard of the Mister South Africa competition, and I decided that Josef should enter. I had him photographed and sent his photos to the competition. As before, Mom was right. Josef qualified for the competition and had to go to the event for the modelling and the interviews. He was a bit nervous, but when he heard what prizes could be won, he got in the car. Josef didn't win, but he came close. He got a modelling contract in Cape Town, but for some reason he never took it up.

The black children were extremely gifted when it came to singing. One could really listen to them all day. They had formed their own choir and would perform at local churches in their rural communities. Little did they know that Auntie Sally was up to her old tricks again, enrolling them in the State Theatre choir competition. Unlike all the other choirs, we had no musical background, and the kids just sang on their own. With my limited savings I bought some material, and I asked a dressmaker to make some shirts for them that would at least be respectable so they could all look the same—look African. She made the shirts, but what a total disaster! Some shirts were too long, some too short, and we were singing at the State Theatre. However, the children's faces had a radiance that lit up the room. They didn't know the dressmaker had slipped up; the fact that someone had bothered to make them a shirt was all that counted. I left it alone and went and sat in the audience.

Listening to all the other choirs, I really didn't think my bunch had much of a chance, but when they all came on, they had an enthusiasm, and those bobbing heads were looking for me. I had to wave, as they wouldn't start until they had this assurance that I was listening. Then I realised that they were singing for me. They didn't care about the other people, they were singing for me. My tears started to flow as they just sang their little hearts out, no accompanying music, nothing. The judges must have realised this, as our little unknown choir with the straggling shirts came third out of all the choirs. Three of the children were picked for the South African Choir, as their voices were totally spectacular. Anthony was begged to sing, as his voice could reach from the base note to the top note of a piano, and the South African choir really wanted him, but

Anthony's heart lay in other areas of ministry. One boy was sent to Switzerland to sing because of his talent, and he did remarkably well there. He now works at the State Theatre. This all came about because we had met at a camp, grown to be fond of each other, seen the talents in them, and told them to reach for their dreams.

Jesus left us a teaching about the four soils.

> A farmer went out to sow seed. As he was scattering the seed, some fell along the path, and the birds came and ate it up. Some fell on rocky places, where it did not have much soil. It sprang up quickly, because the soil was shallow. But when the sun came up, the plants were scorched, and they withered because they had no root. Other seed fell among thorns, which grew up and choked the plants. Still, other seed fell on good soil, where it produced a crop—a hundred, sixty, or thirty times what was sown. He who has ears, let him hear. (Matthew 13: 3-9)

This parable is to encourage the "sowers", those who teach, preach, and lead others to God. I have been going on and on about the wonderful kids, but there were those who fell by the wayside, those who got choked by weeds, and those who didn't have roots. Many nights did I sit up and worry myself sick about certain children, but one can't Bible-bash them. One can only sow the seeds and have the faith that God will do the rest. One can guide, advise, and discipline, but there comes a time where you have to step back and look at what you've managed to achieve.

I always like to read an encouraging poem that by Myra Brooks Welch. It is an apt description of one's life.

> Touch of the Master's Hand
> 'Twas old and battered and scarred,
> And the auctioneer thought it hardly worth his while,
> To waste his time on the old violin.

Many times I have seen the kids as old violins, sitting at auctions almost being sold off for next to nothing. Yet with God coming into their lives, they have radiated happiness, motivation, and determination, upgrading the value of their instrument much more. The tunes and melodies that they actually play out today are melodies I can listen to with pride, knowing their histories and their slip ups, but also their total perseverance to come out on top!

Chapter Seven

TAKING ON NATURE

Besides having camp every year, the children were taught to respect not just the beauty but also the rules of Nature. Some wealthy farmers helped with this, allowing the kids to come onto their various farms and work with the harvest and later the animals.

In the autumn months, the children would go to Botswana and South Africa's border. On the banks of the Orange River was a farmer who would grow endless crops of pumpkins, potatoes, carrots, and onions. The children would have to take off their shirts during the day and assist the farm workers with pulling the vegetables from the earth. This could be a truly tiresome affair, and it required a lot of muscle and on-going strength. The farmer showed no mercy towards the children; they had volunteered for the programme, and he had to get his vegetables to the market within a required period of time. This taught the children that if they were going to go into business, farming, finances, or the like, time was money, and chatting to friends only happened in the evening.

However, farmers and their wives have very big hearts, and the children were always rewarded with the most wonderful cooked meals from the farms. The boys could always chat to the farmers about "men" things, and the same applied to the girls with the wives.

Then there was always farmer fun. The farmers would bring their old Volkswagen Kombis. Everyone would pile in, and the "dare" would be to catch a hare. If you could catch a hare, you got the next day off, plus R500,00. Now, to the kids that was like winning the lottery. The "dare" was on! With a huge spotlight attached to the car and with all the boys really leaning out the doors, they saw the hares. Little did they know how these animals could kick, and kick they did! The children had totally underestimated the balance of Nature, thinking the hares were cute little bunny rabbits that one could fondle. They forgot that God, in His creation, had created animals to survive. Hares weren't cute, fluffy, little animals. One kick could break a man's ribs. That night no hares were caught, no one got the next day off, and no-one deposited R500,00 into their accounts. It wasn't as easy as it looked.

The children were also warned about flirting near rivers. There were no crocodiles there, so what could possibly be the problem? Again, ignoring the farmer's warnings, the children snuck off to the Orange River for a night of what they thought would be romantic bliss. As they listened to the night life, they heard a noise they just couldn't put their finger on. Ghosts? No. They carried on making a noise.

Out of the waters rose a female hippo, most annoyed that she had been disturbed—especially after having just given birth to a baby. (Let's face it, who wouldn't be annoyed?) When hippos get cross, they also get adrenaline and speed from nowhere. Either climb a tree and hope that she doesn't know you are there, or run like mad! This the children did. The boys were a useless at providing any sense of security for the girls that day, as they simply climbed trees, so the girls had to run like mad with Mama Hippo after them. Luckily, hippos only remain on one path, so if you run on a different one, she just makes a U-turn and goes back to her baby. But stay off her path! The children then started to see that God had really come up with an awesome design in the Garden of Eden.

Josef started his first job at the Pretoria Zoo. He was employed as a security guard there, just walking around to make sure that no one interfered with the animals. Every morning he came after his shift to drink coffee with me at the local coffee shop before I started work at the bank, and we would have some quality time together. One day Josef was late. When he did come in, it looked as though he had run from Cape Town to Johannesburg he was sweating so much! The night before, whilst he was walking around bored, a tiger had escaped from its cage. Josef came walking around the corner, and the tiger actually had something to chase for once! Josef had never climbed a tree so fast in his life, and he had to sit there the whole night, waiting for the managers to come and unlock the following morning. One doesn't disrespect animals.

My parents bought an African grey parrot, who they named Paul. Paul wasn't interested in them, he liked me, so much of Paul's life was spent in my house. It was interesting to see how Paul responded to the kids. Lukas was the only one who was allowed to clean his cage, Pieter was the only one allowed to feed him cereal, and Josef was the only one allowed to hold him. He would maul the others if they came near him. He had selected three boys, and that was it. The kids also felt wanted; a bird had adopted them. They would teach him what rugby team to scream for, and when Josef's team played, Paul screamed along with him. When Pieter's insignificant team played, Paul would turn his back on the television set or go sleep.

I have always had a love for birds, and this I taught the children. They knew, even when I went shopping, that the trolley had to have at least eight loaves of bread, as one loaf was just for the birds. I would buy apples for another type of bird that didn't like bread, and make porridge for others. In the garden would be all kinds of food, attracting the different bird communities. I would hear them land on the roof at five in the morning, and by six thirty they were gone, and all the food too. We even started to name certain birds, as they had become so tame they would actually come to the windows and knock for more food. I guess I was trying to teach the children to observe, to watch, and to be patient. Many, due to their backgrounds, had a lot of anger issues, but sitting and watching God's handiwork could be a comfort all on its own.

Someone I know went camping at a site near the Limpopo River. Everyone had turned in for the night, and they were all in their tents, when they heard a lion roar. There wasn't any fear, just caution. However, the lion's roar became louder and louder, and the people then realised the lion was right there in their campsite. The first instinct is to reach for a gun and shoot. God's presence that day calmed the people, saying, "I am here. Just watch." The humans peeped out of their tents and saw the biggest male lion roaring for all he was worth. Suddenly out from nowhere came the entire pride. Then the people realised that he was summonsing the pride. He was calling them for a meeting. This wasn't an attack. This was the king calling. Female lions, male lions, baby lions, all came towards the king. When he was satisfied everyone was there, he got up and led his pride away. When the humans got up the next morning, they saw the largest paw print embedded in the sand. That lion could have killed any one of them with a single big smack. For all they knew, the humans were invading the lions meeting place. The lions knew it, but they just congregated and went somewhere else. Once again, God was at work protecting the lives of the people.

> Daniel answered, "O King, live forever! My God sent His angel, and he shut the mouths of the lions." (Daniel 6:21-22)

The Zulus have a favourite song, which is so significant.

> Who can match Your Greatness?
> Who can know Your Power?
> Who can search Your Riches?
> Who can deny you are crowned, Lord of All?

The Lion will always be King of the Beasts, and God will always be the Lion of Judah and King over all the earth.

Chapter Eight

CHILDREN ARE EXPOSED TO EVIL

I have gone on and on about the wonderful things that have happened, but yes, God had to open my eyes about the seriousness of evil in the world. He also taught me that no matter what lay in store for me, miracles would still happen, as He would be beside me every step of the way.

I have mentioned in previous chapters that my final year students were granted R3000 donations to go on nature courses, whilst I had to look for accommodation for them. These children had no jobs, no way to pay for accommodation, and I certainly couldn't pay for a flat out of my salary. Again I was in a pickle and in desperate times. I knew that among the street kids would the boys would and girls would hire themselves out as prostitutes. All these years teaching them right from wrong would be for nothing if I couldn't make this work. I phoned everyone. No one could help. Again I went on my knees and called out to God in despair. "You know how much I love these children, Lord. Please help me find homes that are willing to look after them until they can find work." As usual, the Lord provided. The bus driver saw me crying on the bus, and he asked me what was wrong. I told him my long story and got off at my usual stop. The next day when he picked me up from work, I heard the news that his family, along with two other families in the neighbourhood, had held a meeting and had decided to take the three boys in for a short period of time. I was dumb-struck. They wanted very little money and agreed to take food as compensation. I had bakeries deliver bread once a week, the meat market jumped in, and a retail shop allowed me to pick up cans of food on a monthly basis. Again the kids were safe. God had worked His miracles and protected us from evil.

There is however, a "but".

But God had me up for some future training that I was unaware of, and totally unprepared for. By now I was working with four children's homes; that's two hundred kids per camp. Then a new visitor arrived on the scene, the Place of Safety. Kids had been placed here by social workers before the courts ruled which children's home the child had to go to or whether the child could be returned to the parents. No one was allowed to visit these kids except selected visitors and pastors, and no photographs were allowed to be taken of the children. I was asked to run a Bible study at this little place for the teenagers, as they were pretty fed up, having being taken out of their comfort zones. The Lord made me go once a week, and the teens and I would discuss various subjects and characters of the Bible. One particular week I sensed the teenagers just weren't cooperating with me, and I couldn't put my finger on it. When I wanted to pray, they would shout and giggle. Then it struck me. There was another presence in the room, and it wasn't the Lord. I was in trouble! I said goodbye to the kids and went to speak to the home mothers. Apparently, three had resigned that week, as they just couldn't handle the rudeness and rebelliousness of the children anymore. This was odd, as these home moms were tough aunties! Then it came out that the kids has started dabbling in the black arts, and some girls had taken demonic call-ups quite seriously. The home moms had left it alone, not realising how it would affect the entire group. The girls had strength of an incredible nature, and they would scream at the home moms with swearing and cursing that no one could take. The only answer here was the Lord. But what could I do? I went home like a dog with its tail between its legs, just wanting to quit. This didn't make sense. God didn't call me for this. He called me for cheerful jobs like camps, singing competitions, and cycling races. Not this! Yet the following week I found my legs heading themselves back in the direction of these scary children. As I waited outside for my turn to do Bible study, I prayed to God for an answer.

It then struck me. My cell phone! I sent text messages to all my friends and family who were Christians, and I asked them to please pray for me at six o'clock that evening night. I told them why, and I felt unsafe. As I walked into that room, the kids just lit up with a cheerful "Hello, Auntie Sally!" and Bible Study commenced as normal. I then felt a different presence in the room, a kinder one. I knew then that yet again another miracle had happened. The Lord Jesus Christ was sitting right next to me in that room, and all that evil was out. The home moms retracted their resignations, saying they would give it one more try. God had yet again, triumphed!

Not all stories ended on a happy note. Joos found his friend dead in her bed after taking an overdose of sleeping pills, whilst writing all over her body that she didn't want to be sent home as she knew her father would sexually assault her again. She would rather die than live through that again. Her plea fell on deaf social worker ears, and this young girl took her own life. Pieter found his friend hanging from a tree, as she was too scared to leave the children's home.

> "Reality" by C. Dominguez
> She's beautiful, she's pretty,
> She's really such a sight.
> Nobody can see by her appearances.

So many times I have walked around shopping malls just for some "me time" and have noticed how parents just drop their children off at the doors, press a wad of cash in their hands, and drive off. I understand that these days many adults are under pressure and sometimes want time for themselves or just want some peace and quiet. That is fully understood. But dropping the kids off at malls? Do you honestly think the kids go and sit quietly in a movie house and innocently eat a hamburger afterwards? I have seen under-age girls being seduced by grown men; I have watched kids walk into the pubs and order alcohol. Nobody cares. Then everyone wonders in utter amazement why the pregnancy rate is so high or why suicide poems like these are written. Children require attention—lots of it. I knew all those children's birthdays. I knew what subjects they had at school and what school they attended, and they weren't even my biological kids. I didn't overwhelm them, but they knew I was watching.

Lukas was arrested whilst waitering in a steakhouse. He was accused of stealing just because he was black. I sued the steakhouse, the police and the entire group for what they did. They didn't know Lukas had a white "mother" looking out for him. However, he still went back to the steakhouse even after all the accusers, thieves and wrong-doers had been fired, resumed his work, and he has been working there ever since.

> That night before Herod was to bring him to trial, Peter was sleeping between two soldiers, bound with two chains, and sentries stood guard at the entrance. Suddenly an angel of the Lord appeared and a light shone in the cell. He struck Peter on the side and woke him up. "Quick, get up!" he said, and the chains fell off Peter's wrists. (Acts 12: 6-7)

Herod's plan, undoubtedly, was to execute Peter, but the believers were praying for Peter's safety. The earnest prayer of the church significantly affected the outcome of these events. Prayer changes things, so pray often and with confidence, believing that God will answer, just like He did with me in the Place of Safety.

Chapter Nine

SPENDING TIME

Even though none of these children were my biological children, I cottoned on very fast to "motherhood". When the kids who seldom had a cent in their bank accounts invited me to "tea", I knew something was wrong.

The first two who invited me for tea hailed from a rural township. They insisted that they wanted to talk "business". When I arrived at the home, these two had arranged an absolutely magnificent spread of food and drinks. It really was a tea! However, kids don't invite you for local chit-chat unless they want something. These two had been very gifted at drawing, and decided that at Grade 6, they wanted to start working for architects and start charging R2000,00 per plan. I had to first come and look at the houses that they had designed. Well, I feel very sorry for the person who purchases the house that these two had designed. It had twenty-seven rooms. It even had a "chill out" room, a billiards room, as well as countless bedrooms and bathrooms. When I asked if they were using tiles or carpets, they said tiles. When I asked who was going to mop all those floors, they quickly changed over to carpets. I then enquired who was going to vacuum this house, and they changed back to tiles, saying that a "Clean Green Machine" had recently come on the market and would assist the buyer. I didn't think much of this, but a month later, these two "dreamers" were hired by a dress-designing firm, where they today work making quite a lot of money. I had encouraged them to dream and use their imagination, and they had listened.

Another couple invited me to tea. Again my hairs pricked up. This time around, Joos told me he and his girlfriend were pregnant. I was most unhappy, as I had always insisted that sex before marriage was wrong. However, a baby was coming, and there was nothing I could do. They got married, and a little girl was born the following year. Little did I know that eight other "grandchildren" would follow! Not by Joos only, but the rest of the kids had found suitors, and they were now at that stage of marrying and having kids of their own.

Whilst going to the Bible study in the rural township, I saw that the kids had snuck a homeless man into the house. This was totally against the rules, and if they were caught, they would get into serious trouble. Most black people have enormous hearts, and they just couldn't turn this young man away. I allowed him to sit in on the Bible study and eat with us. After Bible study, this dirty, smelly, homeless man approached me and asked me for R5000,00. I almost fell on the floor laughing, as he would obviously use this for alcohol and drugs. I wouldn't spend R5000,00 on myself, and here was a homeless chap asking me for that amount!

His story was that he wanted to go on an IT course so that he could get a job later on.

I don't know what happened in that house, but I gave him the money. I never knew him from Adam like I knew the other kids, yet something spoke to my heart and I gave this chap literally all my money. It was about two years later that I was sitting in the bank's coffee shop after a really hard day's work just relaxing with the girls, when a well-groomed black man with a beautiful girl on his arm approached me.

"You are Auntie Sally, aren't you?" he asked. I hate that! Everyone remembers me, but I have that zero-IQ look on my face, because I truly can't remember everyone else. "I'm the hobo from Mamelodi. You sponsored me for R5000,00."

It took a while for me to remember, as all those kids had moved on, and then I recalled the moment. In front of me was the most gorgeous chap. Wearing a suit and tie, he was now a prominent figure in the IT industry, and, true to his word, he had taken my money and gone and studied and was now earning quite a big salary—much more than I was. All this happened because God had worked a miracle and spoken to my heart and hand that night and had allowed my heart to give this chap a chance. I still don't know his name, where he works, or what he earns, but I know he will always remember that Bible study.

Another group of children that I was growing fond of weren't from children's homes were just plain poor; they lived in a community called Tembisa. I used to love going to their schools with my big kids, and we would take the same games that we thought were hits from camp, and we would play them there in the city halls—banana races, cake races, all kinds of musicals, plays, and, of course, food. I could see God was changing the direction of my ministry from sponsored camps to working with poor children who had absolutely nothing. This would require a new strategy, a new way of thinking. Camp had been a fun place where ministry had taken place, but more than just ministry, this was about teaching kids how to survive.

Due to the political climate in my country it was also very risky for a white woman to just walk into a black community and take the "bull by the horns". However, I knew God was with me, and these kids weren't being assisted by the government. They needed someone to speak on their behalf. I realised that in their final year of school, many couldn't read or write; they were just being put through the system. I volunteered as a teacher. Even though I had no qualifications, these teachers were so exhausted that they were taking any help they could get. I would take time off from work, and once a week sixty students would come to my class, where I had compiled worksheets of how to speak and write basic English. They also cottoned on very fast that I was a disciplinarian, and anyone who dared try their luck with me got hit with flying chalk! I wasn't a qualified teacher, so no-one could report me! We prayed for their final exams and for the teachers, as many of them had taken time off for stress relief but had to be back in time for marking. We could see this community really needed God's presence, as outside the school gates lurked the Evil One yet again, trying to sell drugs to those who were trying to get an education or solicit the girls for sex.

Back in Mamelodi at the old Bible study, I had another problem. The Muslims and Jehovah Witnesses were frequenting the children's Homes, trying to get them to come and swap churches for money. The kids really needed food and money, but they didn't realise how sneaky Satan actually was. My only way out was to wait for these chaps to come knocking and Bible-bash them as they came into the houses. The kids would invite the Jehovah Witnesses inside, and Auntie Sally would appear out of nowhere with her big Bible, and we would compare notes. The kids would watch as the stammering of the Jehovah Witnesses would continue, and the more they tried, the more the Holy Spirit fought through me. Game on! Eventually out of total exhaustion, they would scurry out, never to return. The Muslims also came to learn that a Christian woman with a very big Bible was in the house with the kids, so they started leaving the kids alone.

However, when you think you've conquered and cut off the dragon's head, two more heads grow back. Many of the black folk truly believe in witch doctors, and live in absolute fear of them. One of the children, Maria, whom I took under my wing, contracted HIV from her husband due to his adultery. Maria didn't go to the medical doctor and get retro-virals. She went to the witch-doctor. This fool told her she had to go to all four major provinces of South Africa. She had to *walk* to Cape Town and get a litre of sea water. On the way back, she had to get a rock from the Free State. Passing Kwa-Zulu Natal, she had to get a tooth from a shark, and when she was back in the Transvaal, a branch from a thorn tree. Once this was all done in about five years (due to the walking), Maria had to pay the witch doctor R3000,00 (which she wanted from me), to put the concoction together so that the medicine would work.

I almost got in the car and told her to take me to this clown so that I cold throttle him personally and put him out of business for life. Maria knew I wasn't joking. She knew I would break every bone in his body because of the amount of rubbish he had ingrained in her head. I said "no" to the money, she had to go see a medical doctor. She refused again. I watched Maria just get sicker and sicker, so much so that she lost the use of her legs. Eventually, after much prayer, Maria realised that the witch doctor was not the one who was going to save her, with the little money she still had, she hailed a taxi and went to a public hospital, where the drugs were administered for free. Today Maria is as strong as an ox. She has put on weight and has re-gained the use of her legs. Most importantly, she has seen how the witch doctors and Satan tricked her and almost cost her, her life.

Although we might wish to do amazing miracles for God, we should instead focus on developing a relationship with Him. The real miracle of Elijah's life was his very personal relationship with God. That miracle is available to all of us.

> At the time of the sacrifice, the prophet Elijah stepped forward and prayed: "O Lord, God of Abraham, Isaac and Israel, let it be known today that you are God in Israel and that I am your servant, and have done all these things at your command. Answer me, O Lord, so these people will know you are turning their heads back again." Then the fire of the Lord fell and

burned up the sacrifice, the wood, the stones
and the soil, and also licked up the water in the
trench. (1 Kings 18: 36-38)

God flashed fire from heaven for Elijah, and He will help
us accomplish what He commands us to do. The proof
may not be as dramatic in our lives as in Elijah's, but God
will make resources available to us in creative ways to
accomplish His purposes. He will also give us the wisdom
to raise a family, the courage to take a stand for the truth,
or the means to provide help for someone else. Like Elijah,
we can have faith that whatever God commands, He will
provide the means to carry it through.

God knew that my biggest problem at this stage was
transport, yet I always found bus and taxi service available
when it came to serving Him. God knew the kids
needed protection from Satan when it came to Jehovah's
Witnesses, Muslims, and witch doctors, and he knew that
the children's knowledge of the Bible wasn't like mine. Also,
they weren't extroverts like I am, so they would just sit and
listen to all the rubbish instead of actually converting the
non-Christians right there! God worked Elijah miracles in
His own modern day way.

> "Time" by Erin Friedrichs
> The question that is asked most,
> We hear it every day,
> "What time is it?" they want to know.

It is so important to spend time with children. My father,
as busy as he was, would come home from work every day
and bathe my brother and me when we were small. That

was our fun time with him. When we were older, he would wash the dishes whilst we did homework, and he would stand and assist us in this awful stuff they call algebra and geometry. He and I would love to discuss history, and he and my brother would sit and do accountancy together. That was time together. My mother was always around. She was always there when we needed her, and today, even though my brother and I are fully functional and have our own lives, if we need to chat with either of our parents on the telephone, they are always there. This was also true of our in-laws, mine, and my brother's. The same goes for the children that I have in my life. I might live in the United Kingdom now, and they still all abide in South Africa, but by means of emails and phones, we still know how everyone is and what the rugby scores are. Most importantly, if anything bad happens, they can contact us at a moment's notice and we'll be there for them. My time with them was well spent.

Chapter Ten

PERSONAL ATTACKS

However sweet the lives of the children looked, mine was starting to change. Due to economic and political pressure, I hadn't received a promotion in years, so my pay grade hadn't moved either. The cost of living had become much more expensive, the kids were battling to survive and needed money from me from time to time, and life just wasn't like it was when camp number one had commenced. I needed to change things. However, if I resigned, I would lose benefits like the medical aid, and then I would be in deep water as I would have no access to my tablets. The only answer? God. I prayed to the Lord to please come to my aid. "Father God, you know I need money for myself. For so many years I have assisted others. For once, please help me."

I had noticed that other companies had started up at the bank, and one in particular had interested me. Also, the owner of the company and I had a good telephonic relationship. I plucked up enough courage one day to ask him for his email address, which he gave me, and I mailed him my *curriculum vitae*. A week later I had a job with the new company. I was so taken aback that I didn't tell anyone! It wasn't possible! What now? So, to test God I phoned my medical aid's rival group, and an agent came to see me. That day I signed the papers transferring me across to an even stronger medical aid, effective immediately as I was on chronic medication. I then knew God had given me the green light to go. I resigned my job, and because I had worked for the bank for twenty-odd years, I had built up a fairly strong pension. To avoid taxes, I transferred the pension to various investment groups, where they would look after it for me. With a salary now triple what I had been earning, plus a stronger medical aid, a totally new career had started for me.

With my new instructions given to me in my new company, I realised I hadn't been given any staff. The company said I was allowed to hire contract staff for three months whom they would observe (and which I could choose). I had to train the staff and get them bloodthirsty for business. Well, the only "staff" I could think of was the kids. I got Joos and Josef in the beginning, and Stefan, Lukas, and Jo-Ann joined later. All of them had to take the new banking exams which South Africa had released, and all of them passed. They could now go into marketing on behalf of banks, have assets financed, and sign the contracts on behalf of the bank. The kids were starting to understand business, time management, targets, and all kinds of different people. They realised how difficult clients could be, how difficult I could be in business, and they were quite amazed at the personality differences that I displayed between the office and the home. Money was money! Joos and Jo-ann persevered the longest, and they really did well for their clients and the bank. I am truly proud of them. The others didn't do badly at all, but as the saying goes, "When it's too hot, get out of the kitchen!" The others preferred other walks of life and pursued their careers there instead of in marketing. However, they never forgot their banking exams, and today they will smell a con artist or a scam a mile away.

During my stay at this company, I started realising that my epileptic attacks hadn't come for some time. I reached for a calendar the following January and noticed that for a whole year I hadn't had a single attack, quiver, or shake. God had worked yet another miracle in my life, my health! I didn't stop the medication totally, but the neurologists managed to start weaning me off the main tablet which had been the most expensive and was causing an upset at the medical aid, and still I had no attacks.

I became friends with a neighbour of mine, since I had time to find out who was who in the complex where I was living. Once I got to know Clara, she told me that she had stage three cancer but that the doctors were confident that with some chemotherapy they could win this battle. I had moaned so many years about my epilepsy, and here was someone with cancer. Clara also had a personality that simply lit up a room. She was always smiling; she wouldn't let anything get her down. There'd be a knock on the door, and there she would be standing, insisting that I come over for supper. She had just cooked a whole pot of stew and wanted someone to eat it with. Our friendship continued to grow, but she almost fainted when she heard that I had nine children from nine different fathers. When I explained the background, she relaxed and started to get to know all the kids. They also grew to love her, and their "feeling sorry for myself" attitudes started to wane when they realised there were others with more serious problems than they had.

I suppose I should have been grateful to God for everything He had done, but something was missing. The kids were grown now, and I was forty years old and alone. I wanted a husband. I wasn't eighteen anymore. I couldn't go to the university campus like the youth do today or go to the local club. What would I do? The kids had all married, and some even had children of their own. I was the one who was sorry and alone. I went back on my knees and prayed to the Lord. "Lord, I know I ask for impossible requests, but you know how my heart is feeling now. Please send me someone who will understand my background, someone who would be willing to put up with all these kids, someone who will put up with the embarrassment of an epileptic attack should it return, and someone willing to put up with my nonsense."

Clara sent me to a restaurant one night, and there I fell in love with a total stranger. He almost choked on his steak when he learned about the kids, but he took it up as a challenge. That year we got married. Two months later Clara died. Her cancer had reached stage four, and the doctors couldn't assist her any more. Every one of the children attended her funeral, as they knew she had played a key chapter in our lives. Not only had she played Cupid between Shaun and myself, but she had started to love the kids as her own, and they had grown to love her back.

Shaun was immediately accepted by the children. For the first time in years, they had a father figure. Shaun also began to see that my epileptic attacks had stopped, so he agreed to teach me to drive. I couldn't believe it! It felt as though I had just received the biggest Christmas present! The driving started off okay, but then Satan came along and messed up the whole story again. In the six years Shaun had his car, he never had an accident. I had it three months, and I managed to knock off a side mirror and a front fender and scratch the door. Our drainpipe looked as though a camel had collided with it! But the brave mouse marched on. Eventually I got the knack of this whole driving business, and I was given my learner's licence. I was allowed on the road! True, as luck would have it, on the quietest street of all, a four-wheel-drive truck collided with me, as the driver was chatting on a cell phone and not looking where he was going. Who was going to believe me? Shaun was very angry, but he sorted out all the necessary details.

The accident occurred in March of that year. By July I wanted to die because of the pain in my shoulder, not realising it was because of the accident. I was battling to type at work and battling to drive, but I plodded on. Eventually I felt the pain move to my elbow as well. No problem, out came the hot water bottles, and my arm felt relief. Later on the pain went into my fingers, and I had no control over the entire arm. I knew then that this was serious, and I had to go to hospital. This was most inconvenient for me, as I had lots of marketing to do and sales that had to go through. If I mucked this up at work, it would cost me a lot of money. I was just put in a ward with a morphine drip in my arm, and no one could figure out why I was in pain. I was passed around from doctor to doctor, but nobody could help me. Eventually a pain doctor arrived on the scene. He warned me that he could take my pain away but he couldn't solve the problem. I grabbed the opportunity, as I was seeing numbers flash before my eyes and was more concerned about getting back to work than about my health. The doctor took my pain away that night, and I was back home again the following day.

> After this, Job opened his mouth and cursed the day of his birth. He said, "May the day of my birth perish and the night it was said, 'A boy is born!' That day may it turn to darkness, may God above not care about it; may no light shine upon it." (Job 3:1-4)

Many people think that believing in God protects them from trouble, and when calamity comes, they question God's goodness and justice. God's message here is "Don't ever give up" on God just because of a bad experience.

Children never get tired of asking that fateful question "Why?" Yet the question produces a bitter taste the older we become. Children wonder about everything while adults wonder about suffering.

Our age of "instant" has caused us to lose the ability to wait. We expect to learn patience instantly. I know, I'm a *huge* victim here. I love a wastebasket. If something does not have a home in the house, its new home is the wastebasket. The children had to sit me down and in a group very patiently explain that I had been throwing away re-chargeable batteries, blue-tooth, and all kinds of technological equipment because no one had taken the time to explain to me what it was and what it's function was. So it met with the waste basket. Here, the children were very up to date with computers, cell phones, iPads, and the latest technology. I wasn't. So God taught me patience through the children.

Although some pains have been cured, we still live in a world where many people suffer. Job was not expecting instant answers for the intense emotional and physical pain he endured. But in the end what broke Job's patience was not the suffering but not knowing *why* he suffered.

I guess I can empathise with Job here. I was complaining because of the pain in my arm, and because not one doctor could help. It was a total mystery what was wrong with me. It was as if the Devil had done this on purpose and God had allowed it. I didn't have time for this. I wanted a quick cure, to get back to the run-of-the-mill things. God was trying to teach me patience and time, and I had waved it away because I needed to get back to my files and my clients. I completely forgot about the previous miracles God had shown me and, most importantly, that He would provide.

Maybe God was giving me a break? I had been extremely busy with work, the kids were always around, I was married with new duties, and I was totally swamped. God just knew, again, maybe before I throttled someone, that I needed time out. Only when I look back do I see how He worked. At the time I didn't see.

Chapter Eleven

STANDING STRONG!

A common children's song that we always sang at camp and that stuck in a lot of heads was God's Army Song:

> I may never march in the infantry,
> Ride in the cavalry,
> Shoot the artillery.
> I may never zoom over the enemy,
> Cause I'm in the Lord's army. Yes, Sir!

Remembering these words, I can say that being in God's army can be exhausting, but it is also very rewarding. Working with the children and watching them grow up as I did was the funniest time of my life. When boys disappeared, you knew something was wrong. When you did eventually find them, they had taken an enormous sheet, tied a cord on the ends, and were parachuting off the roof of someone else's house. One of the kids was being used as a scapegoat so that not all of them would get hurt, only him. Once the science was right, they would all start jumping.

When romance hit the air, Stefan was asked to a party a hundred miles away. I was most sceptical about the young girl who had invited him, but he insisted he had it all sorted out; he had bus tickets, and all was in order. Sitting at work, I was called to the front desk. Thinking it was a client, I was amazed to see Stefan there, looking like a turkey. He and his friend hadn't organised bus tickets home, so he had to walk. In the South African sun he had burnt to an absolute crisp. He expected love and sympathy. What he got was the entire bank laughing at him. This sounds harsh, I know, but the children had to learn that with bad decision-making came consequences.

However, besides the humour, tears and anxiety came too. The children started having relationships, and I suspected marriage for two of the couples. While I was sitting alone in my house one night, there was a knock at the door, and the young man who was about to propose to Mandy stood there in tears. He and I had arranged that I was going to cook dinner for the two of them, and then I would have to perform a disappearing act and sit with one of the neighbours when he proposed to her. However, he showed Mandy's ring to his best friend, who leap-frogged him and proposed to Mandy the night before. This boy's life was shattered. Here I sat with a chap crying on my carpet, and I quite didn't know what to say to him. Once again, evil had befallen the children.

I then got a phone call from the young folk in the townships, saying that Sipho, whom I had been fond of for many years, had gangrene in his legs. I had wondered where he had disappeared to, and I had heard from his friends that he had gone back to his tribe in Kwa-Zulu Natal. What

I didn't know was that he had been arrested for a crime he didn't commit and had been sitting in prison getting sicker and sicker. By the time the police realised that they had arrested the wrong boy, the infection in his legs had become too widespread and severe, and the doctors had to amputate the bottoms of both his legs.

Another young chap ended up using a public toilet as his new home, as the only family he had was his granny, and she had died from old age. He had nothing and nowhere to go. The Lord and His grace were with TK, and he started working at the youth campsites. Being out there in the nature camps was a true blessing for him. Not only did he acquire food and lodging, but he received an education through Scripture Union, one of the most powerful ministries in the world. Today he is employed as a youth worker for Scripture Union and is enjoying his work thoroughly.

For the whole week the kids would look forward to going out on Friday night. Your age and how you did in school would determine what time you were expected back home. The kids would start getting ready at about six o'clock every night, but one huge stumbling block would always spoil their plans. A new little lady of four years old had been admitted to the home, and she could honestly give Jimmy Hoffa a run for his money. She could disappear so quickly, and then *everyone* would have to jump in and go look for her. She had a problem with people living on the streets. This, to her, didn't look right, so she would take food from the home and go distribute it to the less fortunate. She had a route that she would normally follow, but once she cottoned on that the big cross teenagers would come looking for her, she'd change her route. This would shorten the evenings for the teenagers and lengthen hers. The kids thought locking her in a room would work, but they never thought she could squeeze through the windows and crawl away like she did! They do say revenge is sweet.

Even though these were the sweet stories, the impossible ones lay ahead. Fourteen boys were found to have been be molested by a school headmaster, and this man served on the board of one of the homes. He had molested four of the children I knew, and these kids had gruelling court cases ahead of them. The public was in an uproar. They wanted the abuser's head! At the end of his trial he got sixty-three years imprisonment, which was satisfying to the boys. However, this monster appealed and got off. I never told the boys, as they were still under the impression this man was behind bars. However, one of them started with terrible aggression problems and battled with relationships. The only thing I could do was take him to a psychiatrist. The verdict wasn't what I wanted to hear. My only outlet now was the Lord. Only He could close this boy's mind as to the terrible things that had been done to him and his friends. Today he is in love and has three beautiful children. He is a shining example of how to combat abuse. He loves to be around people, doesn't drink, and has done well in his career. Only God can help in trials such as these.

Lukas eventually asked Violet to marry him, and soon my tenth grandchild was on the way. However, there was another problem. Tribal customs and traditions dictated that Lukas had to pay "lobola" marital fees to Violets mother. This lady wanted R8000,00. Lukas worked ever so hard to get the money together for rent, the lobola, and the new baby. He succeeded with God's help, and on the first of May he phoned to ask me to meet him for a cup of coffee. No "Mom it's a girl! Mom it's a boy!" just "Meet me for coffee." I started to imagine all the most awful things! When he walked into the coffee shop, I could see something was wrong. Children have a "look" on their faces. I just knew their baby was dead. Lukas confirmed it. What I didn't know was that his mother-in-law had taken Violet back to the tribe for the birth and had not admitted her to a public hospital. Violet had taken something that the witch doctor had given her; she had gotten extremely sick, and the baby had died. What hurt these two the most was the fact that they couldn't even bury their baby, light a candle for it, or name it. It was just yanked away by the witch doctor, as its organs would be used for future magic. Violet was declared fit for future fertility production, and Lukas had to pay the money. I was in shock! Utter horror! I think I was crying more than they were. Here Satan was truly taking over. Ancestral descent, tribal ritual, tradition—these all came before Christianity. I had to get down on my knees again and ask God for another miracle.

When we see evil leaders who live long lives and good leaders who die young, we may wonder if God controls world events. We have seen terrible things happening, like the collapsing of the Twin Towers, the tsunami's in the East, earthquakes, bombings all over the world, and unforeseen murders. Daniel saw evil leaders with almost limitless power, but Daniel knew and proclaimed that God "sets up kings and deposes them." God governs the world according to His purpose. The children always used to ask, "Why doesn't God love me? Why does God always allow me to suffer?" My answers were that, just like Job, it was because

God knew they could handle it. It is easy to be jealous of celebrity singers and actors who end up living the life we would so like. However, so many of them have taken to drink, drugs, meditation, yoga, Buddhism, and the occult for peace in their lives, and they still wind up with divorces, suicide, or other sad events in their lives. They may have money, but they are really pretty miserable without God in their lives.

You may be dismayed when you see evil people prosper, but God is always in control. Let His knowledge give you confidence and peace, no matter what happens!

> As I looked, thrones were set in place, and the Ancient of Days took his seat. His clothing was as white as snow; the hair of his head was white like wool. His throne was flaming with fire, and its wheels were all ablaze. A river of fire was flowing coming out from before him. Thousands upon thousands attended him: ten thousand times ten thousand stood before him. The court was seated, and the books were opened. (Daniel 7:9-10)

Daniel, in a dream, saw God judging millions of people as they stood before Him. We must all stand before Almighty God and give an account of our lives. Everyone is trying to establish *when* God will come back and pin a date on it. Thousands of people sold their houses in 1999, as they were convinced the year 2000 was the year of the second coming. Jesus said:

No one knows about that day or hour, not even the angels in Heaven, nor the Son, but only the Father. . . . Two men will be in the field; one will be taken, the other left. Two women will be grinding with a hand mill; one will be taken, the other left. (Matthew 24: 36-41)

Christ's second coming will be swift and sudden. It may be through death from old age, accident, illness, or His actual return to earth. If Jesus and the angels in heaven don't know when God will return, how, through science and planning, would we ever know? Our job is to be always ready for the unexpected. God's plans for us are ever-changing.

Chapter Twelve

DO YOU HEAR YOUR BUSH SPEAK?

If you want me in a good mood, then leave me in peace and quiet with a good book and a cup of coffee. I decided to go the mall one day, order one of those enormous cappuccinos, and just go sit in the corner with my Kindle and read. However, I had one eye on the Kindle and my other was surveying the room. A young girl came rushing in and just sat down on the chair opposite me. No coffee? No hot chocolate? In a coffee house? She didn't even pick up a magazine or a newspaper. This to me spelt trouble, and, up to my old tricks again, I just asked, "Are you okay?" It came out that she was being harassed by a man who just wouldn't leave her alone. She wanted to come see a movie, but he was looking for female company and more. When girls are young, their hormones haven't really kicked in yet and they still have manners. I mean, this poor girl ran to avoid confrontation, but at my age we go looking for it! I was *waiting* for him to come walking into the coffee house; he would have been bludgeoned with a newspaper like never before. I'm not encouraging assault, ladies, please! I'm encouraging you to ask the person next to you if they are okay.

We are so busy these days with dropping the kids off, shopping, going to do our hair, picking the kids up, homework, preparing supper, and projects for school that we haven't a clue what's happening over the road or just next door. I'm not saying that you should become the local busy-body, but just be there for your friends and neighbours. So many people have lost their jobs, and go to bed hungry every night. My friends and I have personalities where we, through years of asking for donations, don't hesitate to walk into shops and organise for other families. But we need to *know* about the problems.

Late at night I heard a knock at the door. In South Africa you go to the door with a cricket bat that time of night! Here stood an elderly black lady who only came up to my elbow, and I had a cricket bat ready to swing! She had heard that I had a mouth on me and I that stood up for people if I knew the situation was legal and true. It turned out that she had been running a business for the town council, but for three months she hadn't been paid. She had no cash to keep going, she was short on food, and she was dead scared that she would lose her tender if her staff stopped coming to work because she had been short paying them. Could I please help? This was a new one—Auntie Sally taking on the town council! Well, she had brought her contract with her, and reading through it, I saw that the council were indeed in breach of their side of the contract. It was time for them to pay up!

I gave her some taxi fare to return to her township, and I went to the council the next day. I found out that the people in charge hadn't registered her as a receiver of money (payee), so she just wasn't getting paid. I made an arrangement with them that all her arrears would be paid to her that day, and because I had a fax machine, proof of the payment would be sent to me. I never went to the council intending to fight, but they knew and could see I wasn't going home until this woman's matter was settled.

God had steered me totally from camp, to raising teenagers, to marrying them off, to teaching them business so that they could have bank accounts and understand taxes, and into the poorer communities, where a different ministry was needed and where there was a another demand. The need was more for time and effort, not for money any more. Whether it was with kids or poor people, I was getting tired. One cannot just go on and on without experiencing exhaustion.

> But those who hope in the Lord will renew
> their strength, they will soar on wings like
> eagles; they will run and not grow weary, they
> will walk and not be faint. (Isaiah 40:31)

Even the strongest people get tired at times, but God's power and strength doesn't diminish. When I felt as though everything around me was about to come crumbling down, I knew I could call on God for strength.

> When the Lord saw that he had gone over to
> look, God called to him from within the bush.

"Moses! Moses!" And Moses said, "Here I am."
(Exodus 3:4)

God spoke to Moses from an unexpected source—a burning bush. When Moses saw it, he went to investigate. God may use unexpected sources when communicating with us too, whether through people, events, thoughts, or experiences. Be *willing* to go and investigate, and be open to God's surprises!

I've always enjoyed the stories of Moses. I'm actually quite jealous of him, as God showed Moses His sovereignty in so many ways. I would have jumped out of my skin if a plant just started talking to me—but I also would have obeyed God right then and there! Moses saw his staff turn to a snake and back again. His arm, after putting it into his coat, attained leprosy, and then it was gone again after he put it back into the coat. He saw the ten plagues and the parting of the Red Sea, and (I think most awesomely) he met with God to receive the Ten Commandments. Those experiences must have been truly amazing! God knew not to put me in charge of any Israelites, because there is no way I would have tramped around a desert for forty years. I would have asked God for directions to the Promised Land and not wandered around like Moses did. I don't think I could have put up with all the complaining either. I would have left the complainers in the desert to die, and anyone who wanted to come with would be free to come. So, God knew what He was doing when He chose and selected those to do His work.

God still speaks from His burning bush. We must just open our hearts and listen. Whether it's a calling to the children's homes, old-age homes, prisons, disadvantaged places, or hospital visitation, God will call you just as He called all the characters of the Bible, and me.

Moses saw a burning bush and spoke with God in visible form. Abraham saw the smoking fire pot and blazing torch. Jacob wrestled with a "man". When the slaves were freed from Egypt, God led them by pillars of cloud and smoke.

The question remaining is "What is your answer going to be?" Is it "Speak, Lord. Your servant is listening." Or is your life too busy with other goings-on to add God to your list right now? As we all tend to forget, God doesn't need us, we need Him. God is not sitting in heaven biting His nails because we are not doing His work. But He will ask us what we bothered to do for the weak, the poor, and those that never met Him because we were "too busy to care" when we die.

What will your answer be?

Lightning Source UK Ltd.
Milton Keynes UK
UKOW05f1057201113

221472UK00001B/2/P